Edited by Helen Exley

To my friend, Pam Brown.
Thank you for everything you've done to help
make this series what it is.

The publishers gratefully acknowledge permission to reproduce
copyright material in this book. While every effort has been made to
trace copyright holders, the publishers would like to hear from any not
here acknowledged.

*Leonard Clark: 'Cowslips' from **Collected Poems and Verses for***
***Children**, published by Dobson Books Ltd.*

*Harry McMahan: 'What is a Grandmother?' from **Grandma was***
***Quite a Girl** by Harry and Gloria McMahan, Escondido, California.*

*Charles and Ann Morse: extracts from **Let this be a day for***
***Grandparents**. Reprinted with permission of Ann Morse.*

Published in Great Britain in 1990 by Exley Publications Ltd.
Published simultaneously in 1992 by Exley Publications Ltd in
Great Britain, and Exley Giftbooks in the USA.
Reprinted 1991
Third, fourth and fifth printings 1992
Sixth printing 1993

Illustrations © Exley Publications Ltd, 1990
Selection & Design © Helen Exley, 1990
Research by Pam Brown
ISBN 1-85015-236-5

Printed in Spain by Grafo S.A. – Bilbao.

Exley Publications Ltd, 16 Chalk Hill, Watford, Herts WD1 4BN,
United Kingdom.
Exley Giftbooks, 359 East Main Street, Suite 3D, Mount Kisco,
NY 10549, USA.

An illustrated

Grandmother's Notebook

A personal journal for recipes, notes
or family momentoes

Juliette Clarke

Those gasps of astonishment, those shrieks of pleasure,
those sighs of delight, lost long ago when your children
grew wise and worldly, are suddenly given back to you
by your grandchildren. What seem to be the same small
hands clutch yours, dragging you from one excitement
to another — "Look! Oh look! Come On!"

Pam Brown

Ladies Smock

Primrose.

Snowdrop.

Violet.

Once a child is born, it is no longer in our power not to love it nor care about it.

Epictetus

Speaking as a grandparent, a baby is a prescription to cure depression — a "monkey gland" for rejuvenation; a substitution for books, television and radio; a baby brings out the love, tolerance and tenderness which has become rusty with the years.
          F. M. Wightman, grandmother

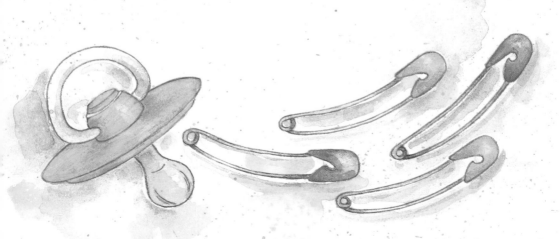

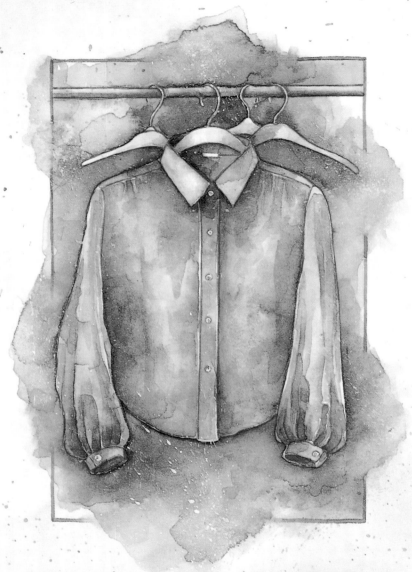

Grandmas are <u>always</u> astonished to find themselves old enough to be grandmas.

Julie B. Jones

*Our grandchildren
accept us for ourselves,
without rebuke or
effort to change us, as
no one in our entire
lives has ever done, not
our parents, siblings,
spouses, friends — and
hardly ever our grown
children.*

Ruth Goode

A baby is a great ego booster to grandparents when needed most — to a grandchild one is considered beautiful, brainy and is implored to sing another song, no matter how poor a singer — and one is made to feel the greatest story-teller of all times.

Doris M. Bridge, grandmother

We are "Just Mum" to our children. To our grandchildren we are possessed of magic, having lived in a time before time began.

M.R.G.

Having grandchildren is the best of all possible worlds. I don't have any responsibility for them — I just do all the fun stuff.

Mary Beth

If anyone had told me I'd be sitting here on a coconut mat, waiting to slide down the helter skelter, I would have said. . . .

Marion G.

I don't go along with all this talk of a generation gap. We're all contemporaries. There is only a difference in memories, that's all.

W. H. Auden

If the very old will remember, the very young will listen.

Chief Dan George

The Cupboard

I know a little cupboard,
With a teeny tiny key,
And there's a jar of lollipops
For me, me, me.

It has a little shelf, my dear,
As dark as dark can be,
And there's a dish of Banbury Cakes
For me, me, me.

I have a small fat grandmama,
With a very slippery knee,
And she's keeper of the cupboard
With the key, key key.

And when I'm very good, my dear,
As good as good can be,
There's Banbury Cakes and lollipops
For me, me, me.

Walter de la Mare

I've never had a posh grandma. I'm glad.

                                    Peter

*There are Respectable Grandmothers and Undignified
Grandmothers. The latter are far more fun.*
                        Eva and Wilhelm Kuper

*Try hard <u>not</u> to drop Gran in it after a day out. There is
really no need to tell Mum you got cut off by the tide. Not
unless helicopters were involved.*
                                Charlotte Gray

*Grans take you on the really fast rides at the fairground
— even if they do go a very funny green.*
                                    Jane Swan

Grans don't mind mud at all not <u>proper</u> grans.
                                J. R. Coulson

Grandmothers try hard, but they run out of puff.
                                    H.M.E.

Grandmothers are inclined to bring their grandchildren home muddy, sticky, radiant, exhausted and two hours late. Wise mothers say <u>nothing</u>.

Clara Ortega

*Grandmothers have the time they never had as mothers
— time to tell stories, time to hear secrets, time for cuddles.*
Dr. M. de Vries

One day we think, at last, we have escaped the ties of children, their troubles and their demands. And then we feel a little tug — and find ourselves bound, once more, by the needs of our grandchildren. And their love.

Pamela Brown

Grandparents are to be thanked
for changing a child's fear of old age
into a thing of strange beauty.
It happens with the grandparent
who gives a child tasty things to eat
or who shows the child old and worn treasures
or who knows how to touch a child as he awakens.
Grandparents are to be thanked
for showing a child, at the beginning of life,
the gentleness of the end of life.

A parent can give a child the stuff of reality;
but a grandparent can clothe that reality
with feelings which make it desirable.
A grandparent's special vision
may not be to see a new world.
But he can know that
the old world was good.
And in himself he can reconcile the
old and the new.
That is a vision worth sharing.

Grandparents will be thanked
for what they have spoken
and for what they have kept to themselves.
The discoveries they have kept silent about,
leaving the child to find his own.
The dreams, the mistakes, the doubts,
the worries, and the fears of old age
they share only carefully with the young.

Yet without these burdens shared,
none has a chance
to grow old gracefully.
Grandparents are to be thanked
for trying anything new,
for the courage to retire
and begin again.

Charles and Ann Morse

WHAT IS A GRANDMOTHER?

Grandmothers don't have to do anything but be there. They are old so they shouldn't play hard or run. They should never say, "Hurry up". Usually they are fat, but not too fat to tie children's shoes.

They wear glasses and funny underwear, and they can take their teeth and gums off.

They don't have to be smart, only answer questions, like why dogs hate cats and why God isn't married. They don't talk baby-talk like visitors. When they read to us, they don't skip bits, or mind if it is the same story over again.

Everybody should have one, especially if you don't have television, because grandmothers are the only grown-ups who have the time!

Patsy Gray, Age 7½

You should not be lulled into a false sense of security by knowing that you are her grandchild. Even grandmothers can be Driven Too Far.
                    Rosanne Ambrose-Brown

My grandmother is very patient. She would have to be with me around!
                    Helena Leeson Age 10

Grandmothers will put up with most things, but they turn a very nasty purple when it comes to Bad Manners.
                    Monique

She has a past of her own and a future which belongs to everyone. She leads an empty life of her own which is filled by the lives of others. Most of all she is a person who will always have time to see you when the rest of the world is busy.

Gill Webb

Grannys are dearly loved by everyone. When your mother tells you you are going to spend a day or two at your granny's you can't wait. When you fall over and cut yourself mummy and daddy are always too busy to put a plaster on. So the only person who is not too busy is granny. At night time grannys tuck you up in bed and make you nice and snug.

Jane Hibbs Age 9

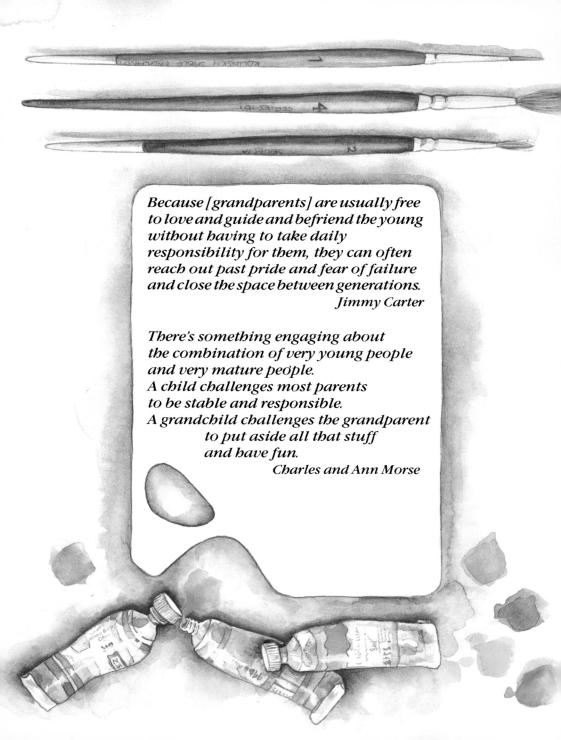

*Because [grandparents] are usually free
to love and guide and befriend the young
without having to take daily
responsibility for them, they can often
reach out past pride and fear of failure
and close the space between generations.*
                                   Jimmy Carter

*There's something engaging about
the combination of very young people
and very mature people.
A child challenges most parents
to be stable and responsible.
A grandchild challenges the grandparent
         to put aside all that stuff
         and have fun.*
                          Charles and Ann Morse

There are two lasting bequests
we can give our children.
One of these is roots;
the other, wings.

Hodding Carter

Grandmothers walk slowly and so rediscover oil rainbows, fallen leaves, puddles and worms in need of rescue.

Julie B. Jones

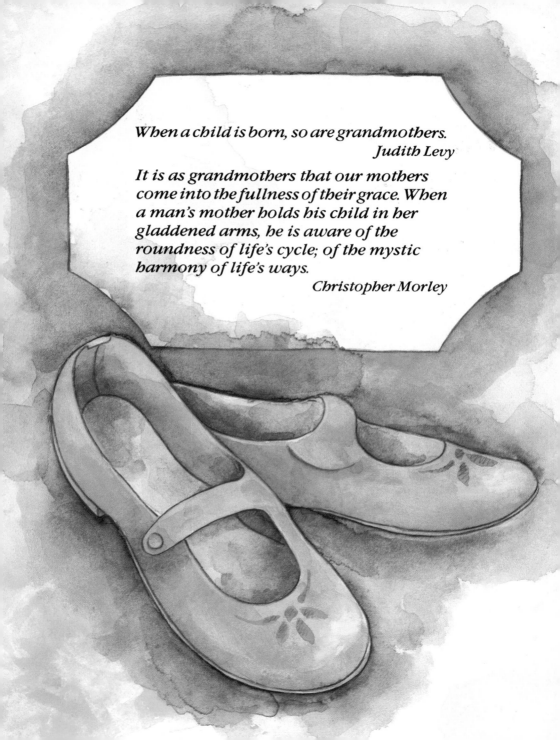

When a child is born, so are grandmothers.
                              Judith Levy

It is as grandmothers that our mothers come into the fullness of their grace. When a man's mother holds his child in her gladdened arms, he is aware of the roundness of life's cycle; of the mystic harmony of life's ways.
                    Christopher Morley

Some grans smell of lavender soap,
some grans smell of French perfume.
My gran smells of pastry and
new bread and peppermints.
My gran smells gorgeous.
                                    Peter

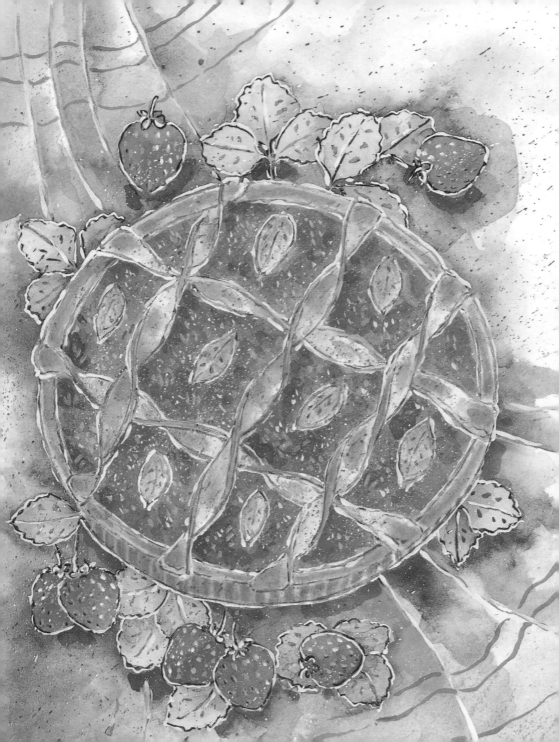

My grandmother makes lots of cakes, but the nicest thing about that is she lets me put the decorations on the top.
                                        Tanya Burch Age 9¹/₂

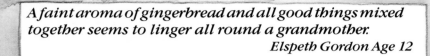

A faint aroma of gingerbread and all good things mixed together seems to linger all round a grandmother.
Elspeth Gordon Age 12

My nanna lets me lick the cake mixture when she is finished. She lets me leave my food, and she spoils me so much that when I grow up I won't want anything.
Sandra Webb Age 10

She cooks delishush diners.
Michael Barbridge Age 7

There is nothing an old woman likes better than to pick up the phone on a dull, dull day and hear the clear, high voice of a grandchild bursting with news.
                                                            Pamela Brown

Long-distance grandchildren always astonish their grandmothers by the way they've changed in only a few months or weeks. But their arms locked about waist and knees reassure them at once that nothing is really different.

                                                            M.R.G.

Far away grans have learned to send love down the telephone wires.

                                                            René Jean Hesse

After primroses, cowslips;
I like the name.
Born overnight in open fields
with new grass, first buttercups;
friends of the clay, they have a secret look.
Their heads catch the sun's gold,
dew pearls roll among crinkled leaves,
bees dust probing tongues in honeyed tubes.

My grandmother loved these flowers,
her mother, too, with the long apron strings,
gathered bunches in these same fields
for winter wine, syrups and creams;
I inherit them now, pick a hundred at a time,
make them into tight balls, as they did,
cowslip balls to hang about the thatched house,
smelling of orange and lemon,
pomanders in spring.

Leonard Clark

WHAT IS A GRANDMOTHER?

A grandmother is a little girl who suddenly shows up one day with a touch of grey in her hair.

Better than anything, she has a way of understanding little boys. Especially men who are grown-up little boys.

Something about a grandmother is always making you hungry. Maybe it's the apple pies baking and the chicken frying and the biscuits in the oven. But Grandma always has the nicest smelling house.

Long before Band-Aids were invented, she was the best person to take care of scraped knees and scratched elbows and banged heads. It was something in the way she touched you.

Grandmother was an expert on mischief, too. Especially when you had been into it. When she looked right into your eyes it was pretty hard to fool her about what really happened. Really.

And it was when you were almost too big to sit in her lap that you began to learn that she was a very special person to talk to. Sometimes, she would give you the right answers without ever saying a word.

How did a little girl ever grow up to be so clever? Maybe it came with the silver hair. Maybe it came suddenly with being a grandmother.

Harry McMahan

Grandmother and grandchild discussing a common interest are exactly the same age.

Duane Birch

There is a frisson that comes when a small grandchild smiles up into your face and says "Oh, thank you for bringing me here", exactly as her mother said twenty years before.

Monique

My grandmother is a refuge. She is a gentle "relic" of the past (although I don't think she would like me calling her that). She is part of the past it is nice to think she has journeyed through the years and is still so sensible and kind. They take care of us, in loving us, but ask for nothing in return.

Susan Philpot

Very tiny grandchildren are allowed to comment on grandma's whiskers, veins and funny teeth. This permissiveness, however, does not extend beyond the age of five.

Helen Thomson

Grans never notice that they have become old until their grandchildren subject them to a detailed examination. Having carefully noted wrinkles, whiskers, brown blotches, silver hair, blue veins and drooping jowls, they comment, with great kindness; "You're <u>very</u> old, aren't you, grandma?". When, of course, it's time at last to admit it.

Pam Brown

We all know grandparents whose values transcend passing fads and pressures, and who possess the wisdom of distilled pain and joy.

Jimmy Carter

*You can get a lot of extra mileage
out of a grandmother
if you let her have a cup of tea.*
Charlotte Gray

Every grandmother has a drawerful of strange crayon drawings and oddly spelled letters that she wouldn't swap for the Kohinoor diamond.

Marion G.

Grandmas have peculiar habits. It's their age.

Paddy

Juliette Clarke
1990

Upstretched arms make grandmas put off rheumatism till tomorrow.

Julie B. Jones

Time has taken edge of vision,
ears' perception, hands' precision
yet how can any feel bereft
when wonderment and love are left?

Pam Brown

A grandma is old on the outside and young on the inside.
John Wright Age 7½
from "Grandmas and Grandpas"

I can remember comparing my grandmother's veined, knotted, brown-splotched hands with my own — of which I was inordinately proud. So little time ago, yet now, here I am with my grandmother's hands.

Pam Brown

Grandmas should write down the stories of their lives, however dull they seem to them. For such tales show history as it is — a procession of interlocking lives. A unity. The family of mankind.

Charlotte Gray

Nana tell tales that she told to mother when she was a child. Many stories of exciting adventures that happened a long time ago. They did not have the luxuries that we have, but dancing the Lancers in their large living room when the furniture was pushed aside, singing round the piano, telling stories by the blazing fire whilst they ate hot muffins. Skating on the frozen park lake in the winter, riding on the top of an open deck tram car, all these more than make up for television and holidays abroad. I hope my Nana will stay with me for a long time, and when I have the farm I long for, she will be able to live with me and feed the chickens. We will have a blazing log fire and she will tell us stories of the past.

Dawn Williams Age 10

Mothers, flustered, busy, distracted, inadvertently bring sorrow to their children. Grandmothers have had time to look back and see their own blunders clearly—and now they watch their children making the same, sad mistakes. All they can do is make a refuge in their hearts where a grandchild can find breathing space and comfort.

Pam Brown

Gran simply never noticed dress or status or skin. She did not choose to ignore such issues out of religious or political conviction. She just didn't notice them. She only saw the individual. It was her best legacy.

Charlotte Gray

July 5th, 1868: Today I have completed sixty-four Springtimes . . . And now here I am, a very old woman, embarked on my sixty-fifth year. By one of those strange oddities in my destiny, I am now in much better health, much stronger, much more active, than I ever was in my youth. . . . I am troubled by no hankering after the days of my youth: I am no longer ambitious for fame: I desire no money except insofar as I should like to be able to leave something to my children and grandchildren. . . . This astonishing old age . . . has brought me neither infirmity nor lowered vitality.

Can I still make myself useful? That one may legitimately ask, and I think that I can answer 'yes.' I feel that I may be useful in a more personal, more direct way than ever before. I have, though how I do not know, acquired much wisdom. I am better equipped to bring up children. . . . It is quite wrong to think of old age as a downward slope. One climbs higher and higher with the advancing years, and that, too, with surprising strides. How good life is when all that one loves is aswarm with life!

Letter from George Sand to a friend

seeds....

ornamental
Gourds —

March

GOURDS

GOURDS

It is too late! Ah nothing is too late
Till the tired heart shall cease to palpitate.
Cato learned Greek at eighty; Sophocles
Wrote his grand Oedipus and Simonides
Bore off the prize of verse from his compeers
When each had numbered more than four-score years...
Chaucer, at Woodstock with the nightingales,
At sixty wrote the Canterbury Tales:
Goethe at Weimar, toiling to the last,
Completed Faust when eighty years were past.
These are indeed exceptions; but they show
How far the gulf-stream of our youth may flow
Into the artic regions of our lives...
For age is opportunity no less
Than youth itself, though in another dress
And as the evening twilight fades away
The sky is filled with stars, invisible by day...

Henry Wordsworth Longfellow

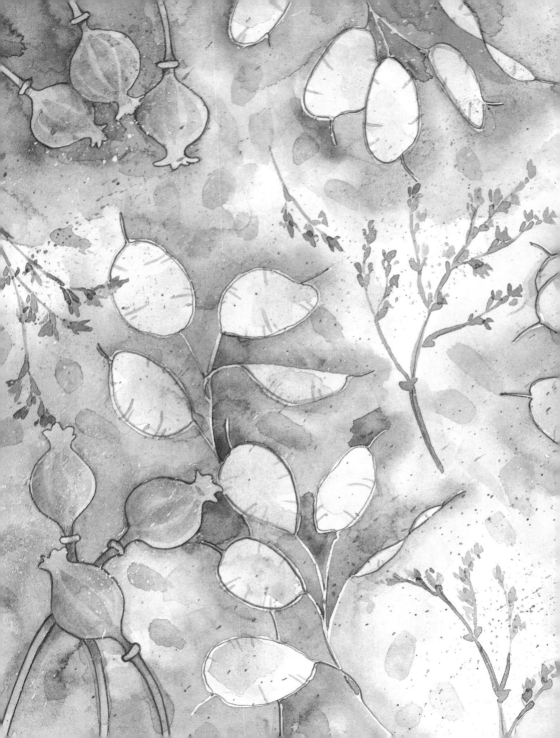